Better Homes and Gardens®

The Princess and The Pirates

A pirate ship sailed quietly into Sands Cove and then disappeared behind Wolf Island while Max and his friends were building sand castles. But no one saw it.

They didn't see the small rowboat when it landed at the beach either. And no one saw the pirates when they grabbed their picks and shovels, and quickly headed for the trees near the beach.

The first one to notice *anything* was Sara Jo. "Look," she called, pointing to a brightly colored bird that had landed a few feet away. "It's a parrot!"

"Where did it come from?" asked Elliot.

"It probably escaped from a pet store," said Max. "Or from someone's house."

"Or maybe it belongs to pirates!" said Sara Jo.

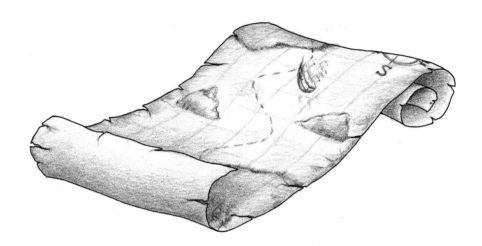

Vera laughed and flipped one ear over her shoulder. "Don't be silly," she said. "Everyone knows there aren't pirates around anymore. I don't know where you get such *ridiculous* ideas! I suppose you think there's buried treasure around, too!"

"What does the parrot have in its bill?" asked Bruno.

"It looks like rolled-up paper," said Sara Jo. "Maybe it's a treasure map!"

"Awwwkk! Treasure!" cried the parrot, dropping the paper.

Bruno and Elliot both scrambled for it. Elliot was faster. "Wow!" he said as he unrolled it. "This *is* a treasure map!"

Everyone crowded around to see.

"Look," said Max. "The map shows a trail that leads to the woods. There's even a spot marked with an X."

"I wonder if it means the woods over there," Elliot said.

"Could be," said Max.

Sara Jo rubbed her hands together. "Buried treasure," she said. "Let's dig it up . . . just like real pirates!"

"But I don't *want* to play pirates!" said Vera. She stamped her foot. "We were going to play castle, and you *promised* I could be the princess!"

"We can do that some other time," said Elliot. "Now we have to look for the treasure."

"Right! Let's go," said Max. And they all ran toward the big rock where Max said the trail began. Everyone, that is, but Vera.

"Well, fine!" Vera yelled after them. "I'll just be a princess by myself!" And she gave the ground a kick. Sand flew into the air and with it, something round and shiny. "That looks like a gold coin," Vera thought as she leaned over to pick it up. But before Vera could grab it, the parrot flew down and snatched up the coin in its bill. Then off it flew toward the woods.

"Hey! That's mine," Vera shouted. "I saw it first!"

But the parrot disappeared into the trees. So Vera followed.

The woods were dark and gloomy. The parrot was nowhere to be seen. Off in the distance, Vera could hear voices, so she followed the sound. There wasn't a path and Vera found it hard to walk.

She kept tripping over rocks and tree roots. "This is no place for a princess," Vera muttered to herself. But she kept walking anyway. The farther Vera went, the louder the voices got. Soon she was very close.

Vera crouched down and hid behind some bushes. Slowly she parted the branches and peeked through, almost afraid to breathe. Suddenly, Vera screamed and quickly turned and ran. For there, looking back at her, was a pirate!

Vera ran faster than she had ever run before. She didn't stop until the woods were far behind her. But she could still hear footsteps and the loud shouting getting closer.

When she reached the beach, she saw her friends. "Pirates!" she yelled. "We've got to get out of here. They're coming this way!"

But before anyone could move, the pirates burst out of the woods.

Vera hid behind Max and covered her eyes. "I'm scared!" she whimpered.

"Why?" asked Max. "They look friendly to me."

And when Vera looked, the pirates she thought were so scary were smiling.

The captain stepped forward. He removed his feathered hat and bowed. "My thanks to you, kind lady," he said. "Squawk, our parrot, flew off with our map and we couldn't find our way out of the woods. We were lost, but then you came to our rescue."

"Lost! Awwwkk! Lost!" cried Squawk.

The pirate bowed once more. "Thanks to you, we can now return to our ship."

"What ship?" asked Max.

"Why, that ship," said the pirate, pointing to the large sailing vessel that had appeared in the cove once more.

The captain called for his treasure chest. "Before we go, I'd like to thank the young lady with a gift."

Vera blushed. "Oh, no! I couldn't . . . "

But the pirate interrupted her. "Please, think of it as something to remember us by," he said.

The pirate raised the treasure chest's squeaky lid and pulled out a beautiful necklace. He handed it to Vera. "Something for a princess," he said. "And for her friends, a little something, too."

The pirates packed up their treasure chest
and carried it down to the beach. They
pulled a small rowboat from its hiding place
behind some rocks. Then with a wave of the
captain's hand, the pirates rowed out to their
ship.

Vera and her friends watched as the
pirates climbed aboard. Everyone waved
until the ship disappeared from view.

Vera looked at her necklace. "He said it
was for a princess," she said in a dreamy
voice.

"Yeah," said Bruno. "But no one will ever
believe where you got it."

"But *I'll* know," said Vera.

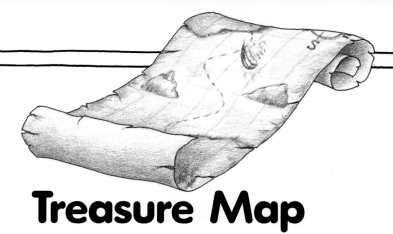

Treasure Map

Follow the secret path made of lemon juice to the pirates' buried treasure.

What you'll need...

- Crayons or colored pencils
- 1 piece of paper
- Lemon juice
- 1 small bowl
- 1 cotton swab
- 1 old towel
- Iron

1 Use crayons to draw a picture on the paper (see photo). Imagine your picture is a map that shows where a pretend treasure is buried.

2 Put some lemon juice in the small bowl. Dip the cotton swab into the lemon juice. Use it to draw a path on your picture leading to the buried treasure (see photo). Let your picture dry completely. (When the lemon juice dries, the path will be invisible.)

3 To make the path reappear, ask an adult to iron the picture for you. Place an old towel on a flat surface. Turn map upside down on towel. Iron picture with a dry iron on low to medium heat (see photo). The lemon juice lines will darken after 10 to 20 seconds.

Pirate Hat

Ahoy, mate! Pretend you're a pirate and wear a folded-paper pirate hat.

What you'll need...

- One 18x24-inch piece of newspaper or brown paper bag
- Tape
- Crayons or markers
- Feathers (optional)

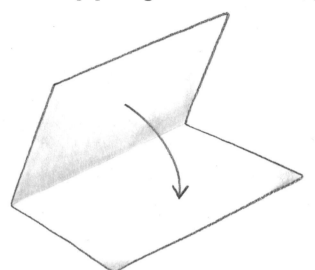

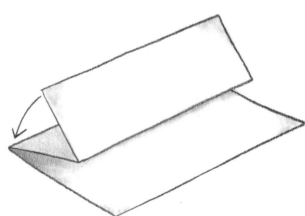

1 Place the paper with a short side in front of you. Fold the paper in half with the short sides together.

2 Fold the top layer of the paper in half. Turn the paper over. Fold the remaining layer in half. Open the paper at the center fold.

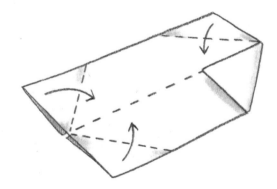

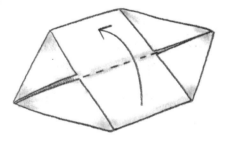

3 Turn the paper over so the flaps are on the bottom side. Fold one corner to the center fold, forming a triangle. Repeat with the 3 remaining corners.

4 Fold the paper in half lengthwise so the corners are enclosed in the hat. Tape the top edges of the hat together. Decorate the hat with crayons. If you like, tape on feathers.

Spyglass Sandwiches

Be on the lookout for lunch so you can try these fun-to-eat sandwiches.

What you'll need...

- Ingredients for Ham and Cheese Filling or Peanut Butter Filling (see page 32)

- 1 small bowl
- Wooden spoon
- Table knife

- 8 slices of bread
- Rolling pin
- Measuring spoons

1 Put all the ingredients for the Ham and Cheese Filling in the small bowl (see photo). Stir with the wooden spoon and mix everything well.

2 Use a table knife to cut the crust off each slice of bread. Flatten each slice lightly with the rolling pin or your hand. Spread about *2 tablespoons* of the filling on 1 slice of bread (see photo). Repeat with remaining filling and bread.

3 Beginning with 1 long side of a slice of bread, tightly roll up the bread (see photo). Repeat with remaining bread. Serve immediately or wrap tightly with clear plastic wrap. Chill up to 24 hours. Makes 8 sandwiches.

Pirate Hat

Real pirates wore hats like the paper-folded hats pictured on page 28, except the pirates' hats had three corners. This kind of hat was called a *tricorne*, or three-cornered hat. Here are some more words you can learn about pirates.

● *Booty* was the treasure pirates stole from other ships.

● *Buccaneer* is another name for a pirate.

● A *Jolly Roger* was the flag on a pirate ship. Every ship had its own symbols on its flag. A pirate flag with a skull and crossbones is a well-known Jolly Roger.

● When pirates captured a ship, they called it a *prize*.

Treasure Map

Here are some fun facts about pirates and how they found their treasures.

● Pirates sailed on ships many years ago. They sailed the seas looking for other ships that carried gold and jewels or other things worth a lot of money. If they found one, the pirates would capture the ship and take its treasures.

● Men and women who became pirates thought they could get rich quick. But that didn't happen very often. When pirates captured a treasure, sometimes they would bury it. But most of the time, they would spend their money right away.

Spyglass Sandwiches

Pick either of these fillings for your Spyglass Sandwiches. Then follow the directions on page 31 to put them together.

● Ham and Cheese Filling

  1 4½-ounce can deviled ham
  1 3-ounce package cream cheese, cut up and softened
  2 tablespoons chopped green pepper or celery
  1 tablespoon chopped pimiento (optional)
  ½ teaspoon prepared mustard

● Peanut Butter Filling

  ½ cup soft-style cream cheese
  ½ cup peanut butter
  ¼ cup shredded apple or carrot

A spyglass is like a telescope. When you look through it, you can see faraway things up close. If you like, use a paper towel tube or a toilet paper tube for a pretend spyglass.

BETTER HOMES AND GARDENS® BOOKS
Editor: Gerald M. Knox   Art Director: Ernest Shelton   Managing Editor: David A. Kirchner
Family Life Editor: Sharyl Heiken
THE PRINCESS AND THE PIRATES
Editors: Jennifer Darling and Sandra Granseth   Graphic Designers: Harijs Priekulis and Linda Vermie
Project Manager: Liz Anderson
Contributing Writer: Nancy Buss   Contributing Illustrator: Buck Jones
Contributing Color Artist: Sue Fitzpatrick Cornelison   Contributing Photographer: Scott Little

Have BETTER HOMES AND GARDENS® magazine delivered to your door.
For information, write to: ROBERT AUSTIN, P.O. BOX 4536, DES MOINES, IA 50336